AF484497

ARISTURTLE©

THE SAYINGS OF ARISTURTLE

WITHIN THESE PAGES YOU WILL FIND THE FIRST COLLECTION OF THE SAYINGS OF ARISTURTLE.

THE SAYINGS ARE NOT CHRONOLOGICALLY ORGANISED. ARISTURTLE HIMSELF HAS QUESTIONED THE RELEVANCE OF TIME AS A WAY TO ORDER THINGS.

EACH SAYING SHOULD BE READ QUIETLY TO ONESELF AND CONTEMPLATED BEFORE MOVING ON TO ANOTHER SAYING.

ON THE OTHER HAND, YOU CAN READ ALL OF THEM IN ONE GO AND YOU CAN DO THIS ALOUD AS WELL.

ARISTURTLE DOES NOT SEEM TO CARE ENOUGH EITHER WAY!

SO, ENJOY THESE SAYINGS. I HOPE THAT I HAVE SCRIBED THEM AS FAITHFULLY AS I HEARD THEM THE FIRST TIME.

AND WHILE ARISTURTLE IS PAINFULLY CAMERA SHY AND NOT GIVEN TO PORTRAITURE, MY FRIEND DEBU HAS TRIED TO CAPTURE HIS ESSENCE IN THE ACCOMPANYING ILLUSTRATIONS.

SHANTABABA

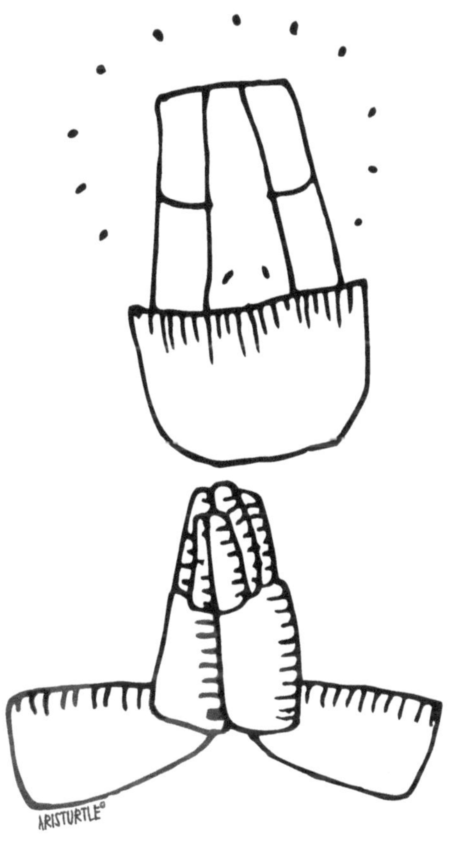

MAYBE WE ARE ALL HERE JUST FOR THE TIME BEING.

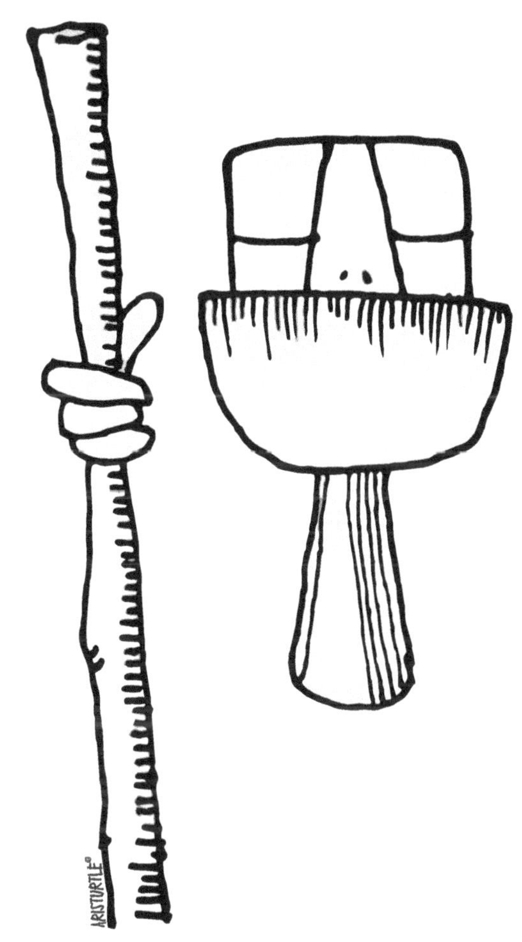

WHEN I AM PATIENT, I FIND THAT I HAVE
NO NEED TO HURRY.

UNDERNEATH ALL THE SHELLS, KNOWING ME IS KNOWING YOU AND KNOWING YOU IS KNOWING ME.

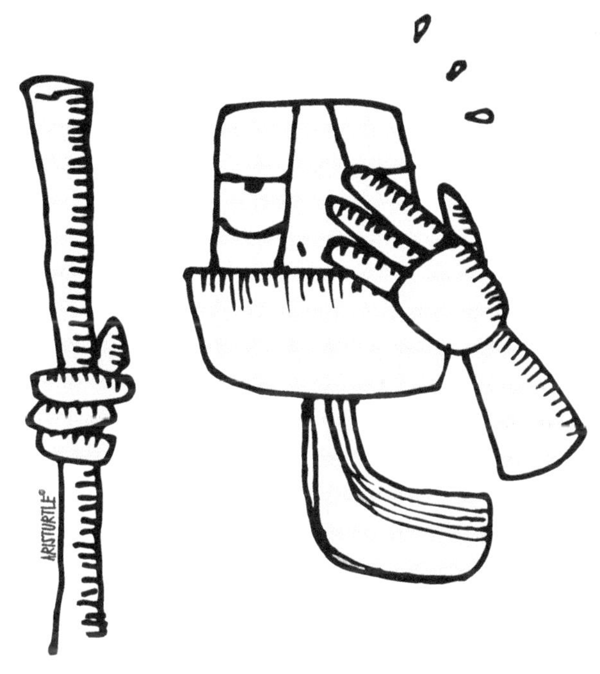

SOME DAYS I HAVE MIXED FEELINGS ABOUT
THE WORLD NOT ENDING.

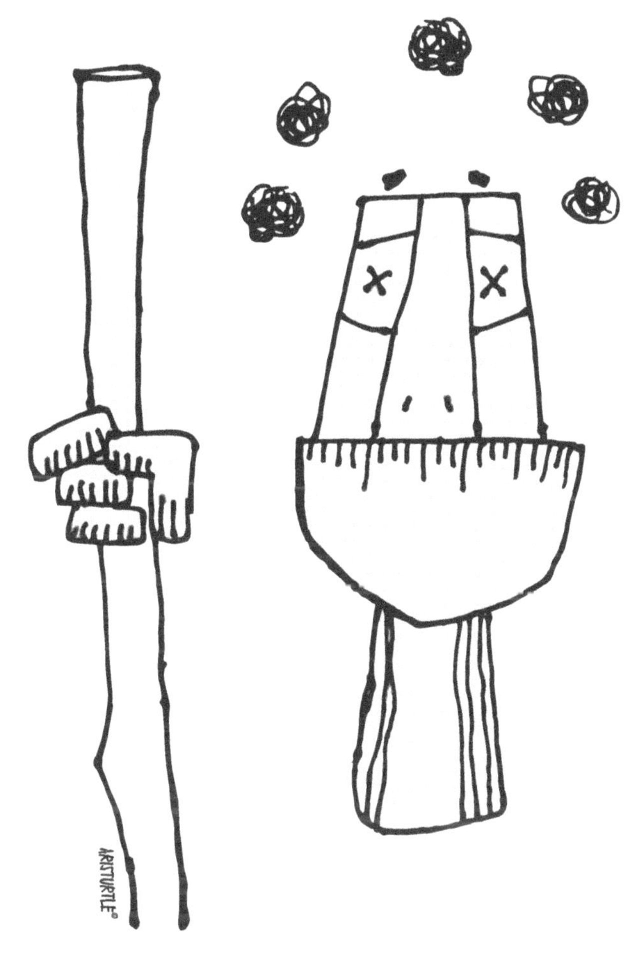

I HAVE COME TO UNDERSTAND THAT SHELL SHOCK IS JUST AN EUPHEMISM FOR A BRUISED EGO.

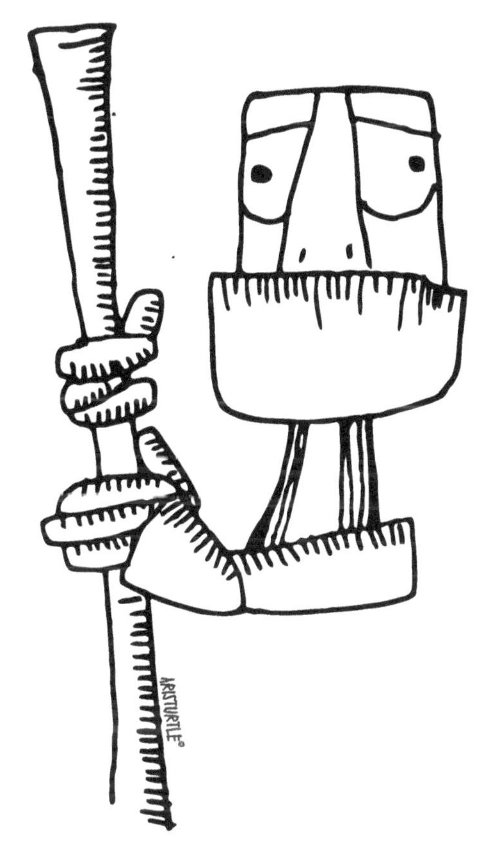

SHOULD I TURN LEFT? OR GO RIGHT? I DON'T LIKE POLITICS. SO I THINK I WILL JUST STAND RIGHT HERE.

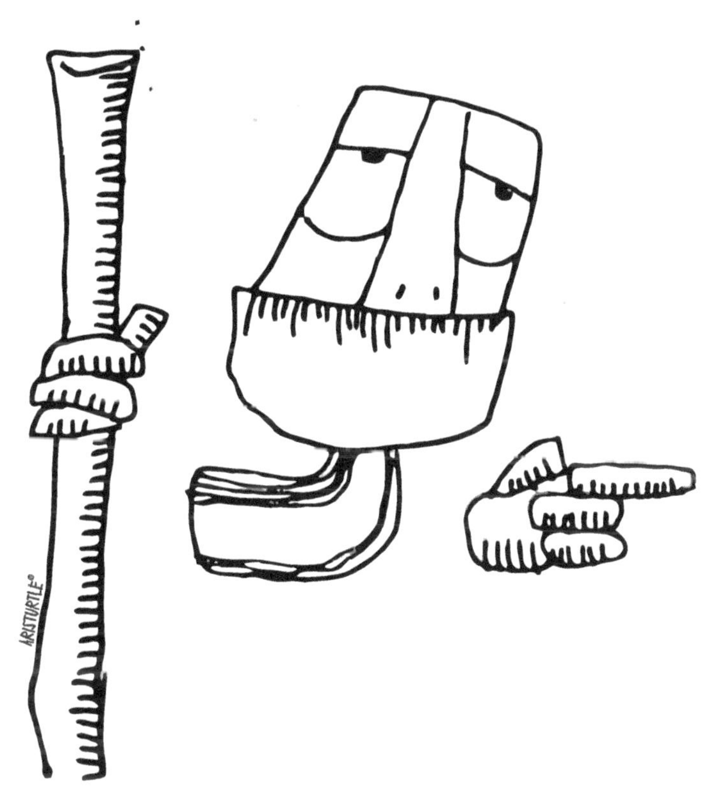

I FOLLOW NO ONE. I JUST CANNOT SEEM TO KEEP UP.

I WONDER AS I WANDER.
MAYBE I WONDER BECAUSE I WANDER.

IT IS NOT HOW FAR YOU TRAVEL BUT WHETHER YOU MADE EACH STEP COUNT.

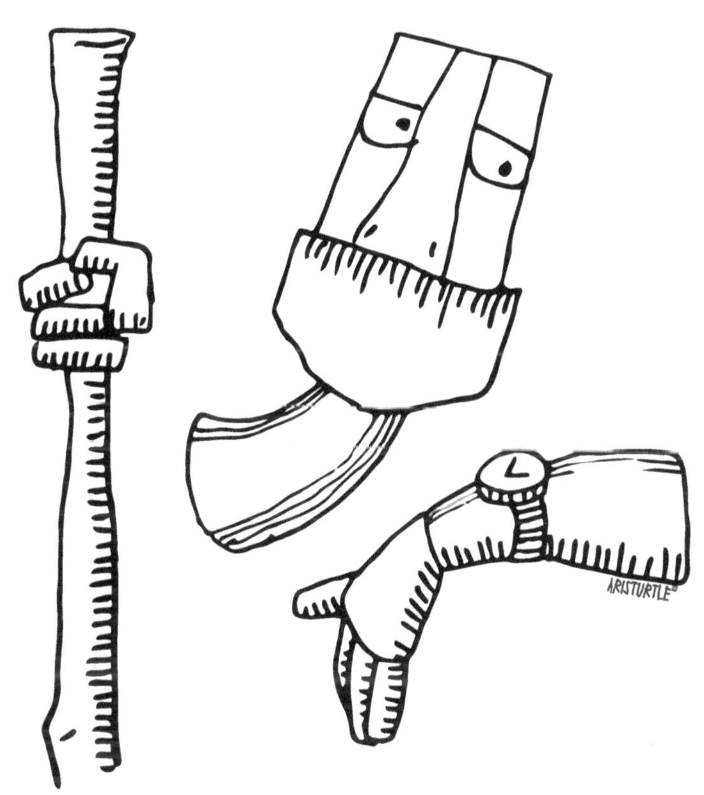

I THINK I HAVE CONQUERED TIME.
I CANNOT GO FAST SO I RELISH EACH MOMENT.

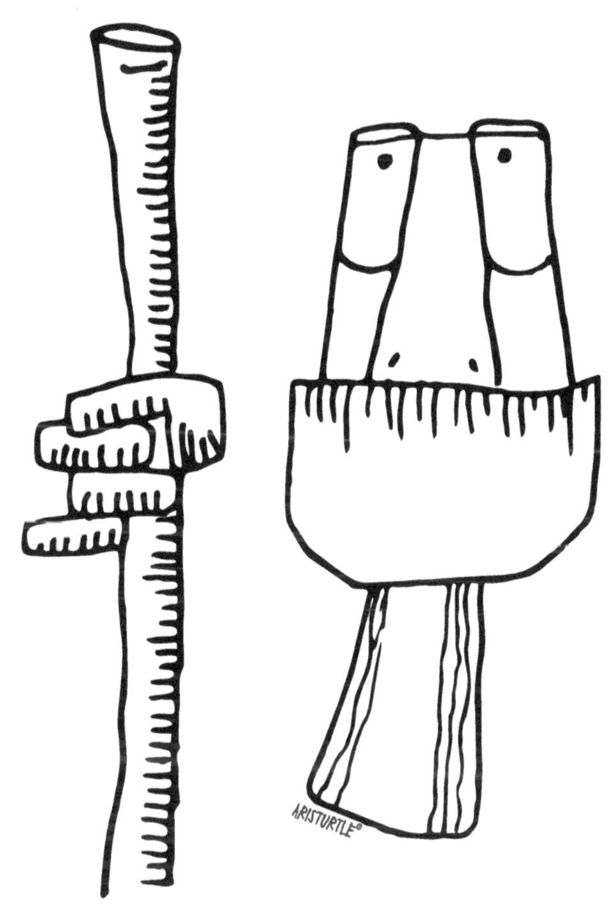

SURE I HAVE OPINIONS. I SPEND SO MUCH TIME THINKING ABOUT THEM THOUGH, THAT OFTEN I CHANGE MY MIND.

DOES LAUGHTER HEAL SADNESS? YES IT DOES.
ONCE YOU START LAUGHING.

I LIKE IT WHEN PEOPLE TELL ME I AM HARD ON THE OUTSIDE AND SOFT INSIDE.

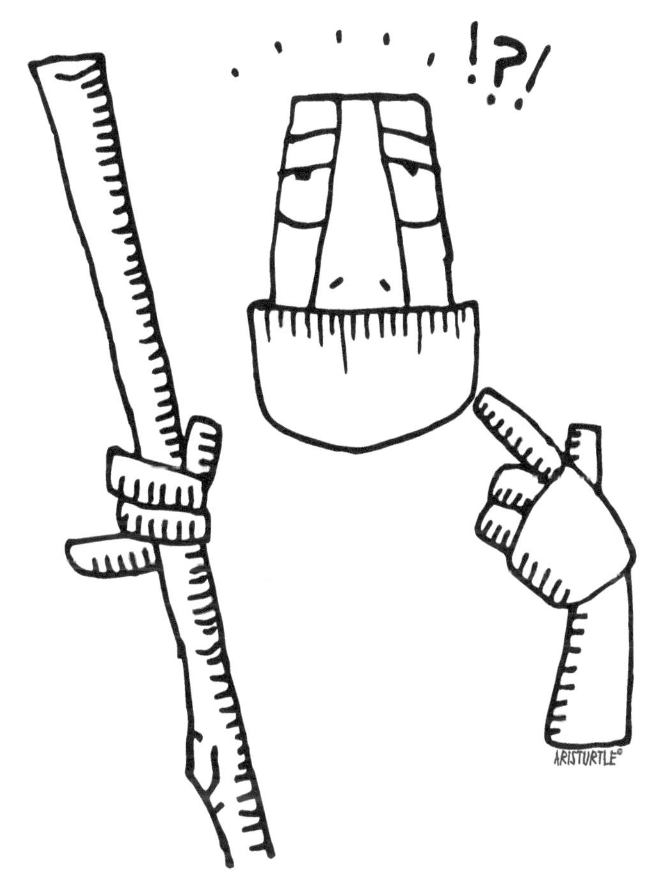

WHO REALLY KNOWS WHO CREATED THIS WORLD. LOOKING AT ME, I THINK HE HAD A GREAT SENSE OF HUMOUR

SOME PEOPLE TELL ME THAT I AM OBSESSED WITH TIME.
OF COURSE I AM. TIME IS ALL I HAVE.

FOR SOME MONTHS NOW I STOPPED SPEAKING.
I HAD NOTHING TO SAY.

SOME DAYS I FIND MYSELF STUCK IN WINTER WHEN SPRING HAS ALREADY ARRIVED.

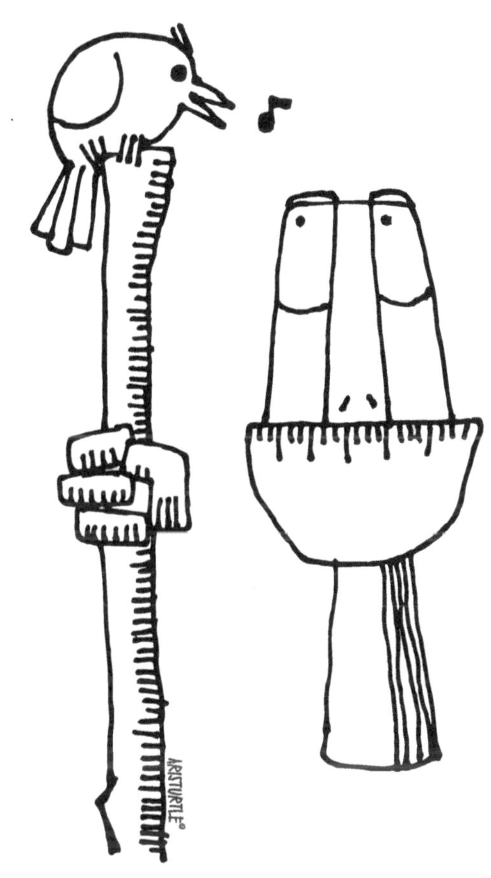

I REALLY ADMIRE BIRDS. FROM MY POINT OF VIEW THEY LOOK CAREFREE. I WONDER WHAT THEY THINK OF ME.

WHATS THE BEST FRIEND YOU EVER HAD?
FOR A LONG TIME, FOR ME, IT WAS A ROCK, THAT LOOKED
JUST LIKE ME.

I HAVE A STATELY MEASURED TREAD.
PEOPLE HAVE SAID THAT I LOOK LIKE ROYALTY.

ONCE I MET A LARGE SNAIL GOING THE OTHER WAY.

WE HAD TIME FOR A REALLY LONG CONVERSATION BUT WE WERE TOO SHY TO SAY HI.

DO YOU REALLY WANT TO RUSH TO YOUR DESTINATION?
I NEVER SEEM TO HAVE THAT PROBLEM.

BECAUSE I SPEND A LOT OF TIME LOOKING AT THINGS,
TIME SLOWS DOWN FOR ME

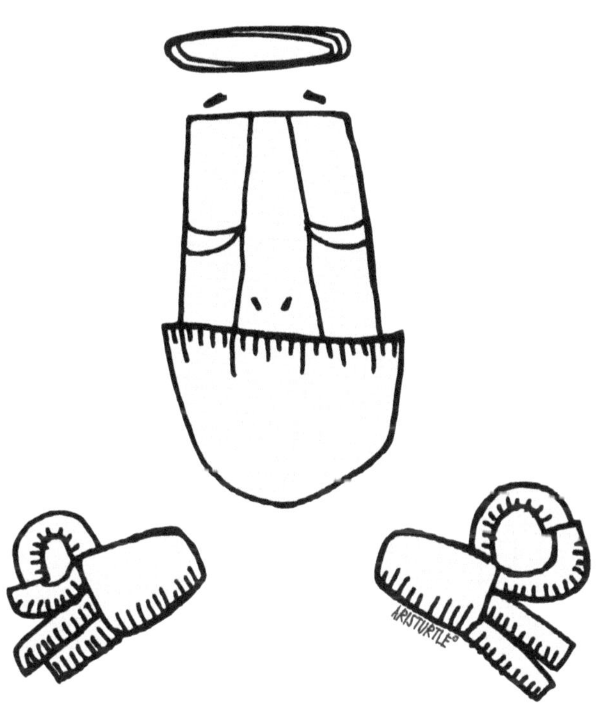

I AM NOT SURE THAT I WANT TO LIVE AS MUCH AS THEY SAY I CAN LIVE. I AM NOT SURE I CAN KEEP LEARNING FOR THAT LONG.

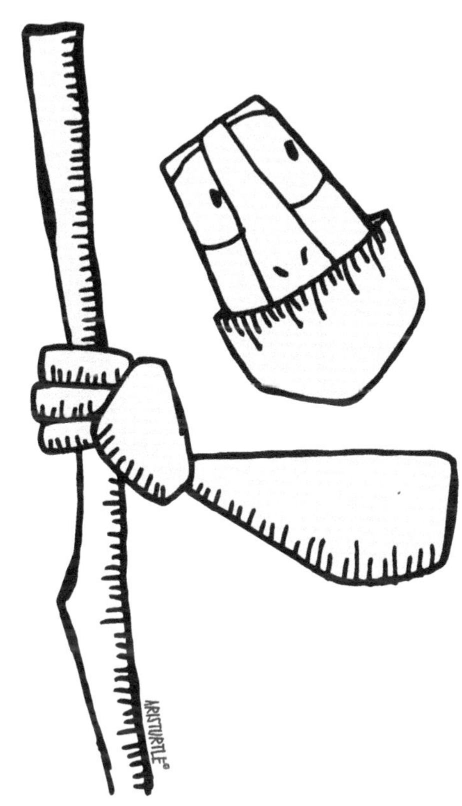

THE MORE I GET SOMEWHERE, THE MORE I HAVE TO GO SOMEWHERE.

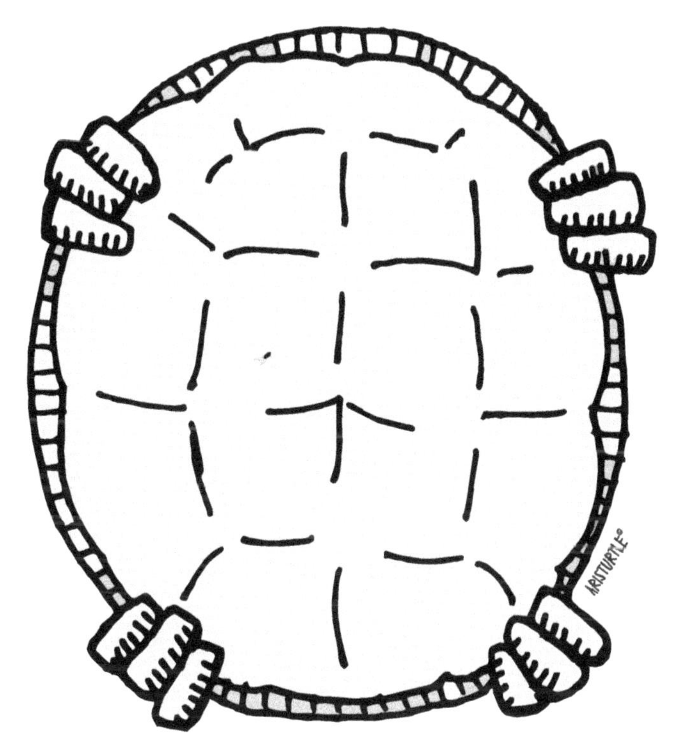

EVERYONE SHOULD RETREAT INTO THEIR SHELL. IT'S THE ONE PLACE YOU CAN MAKE SENSE OF WHAT'S OUTSIDE IT.

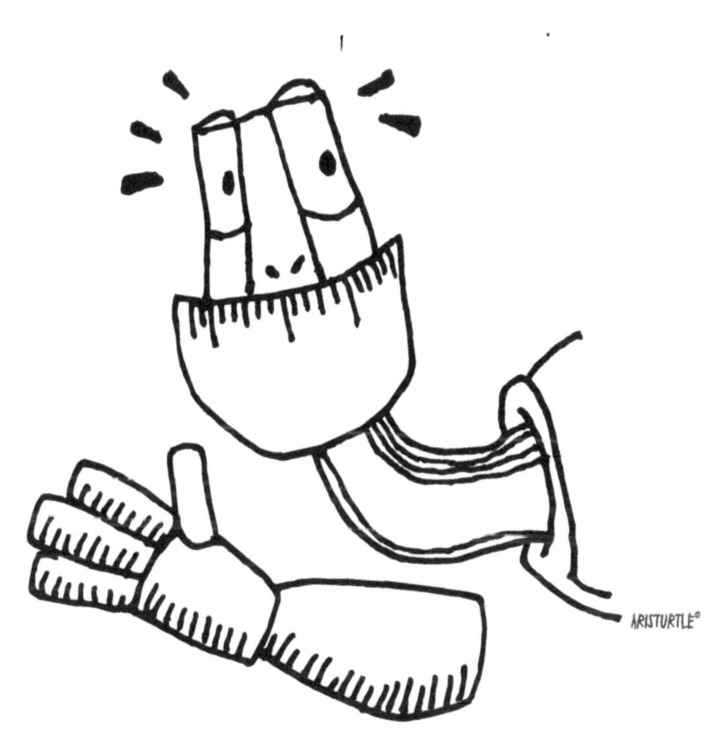

IT'S ONLY WHEN I STICK MY NECK OUT, THAT I CAN SEE
THE WORLD IN FRONT OF ME.

I MOSTLY EAT LEAVES. IT DOESN'T MEAN THAT
I WON'T BITE.

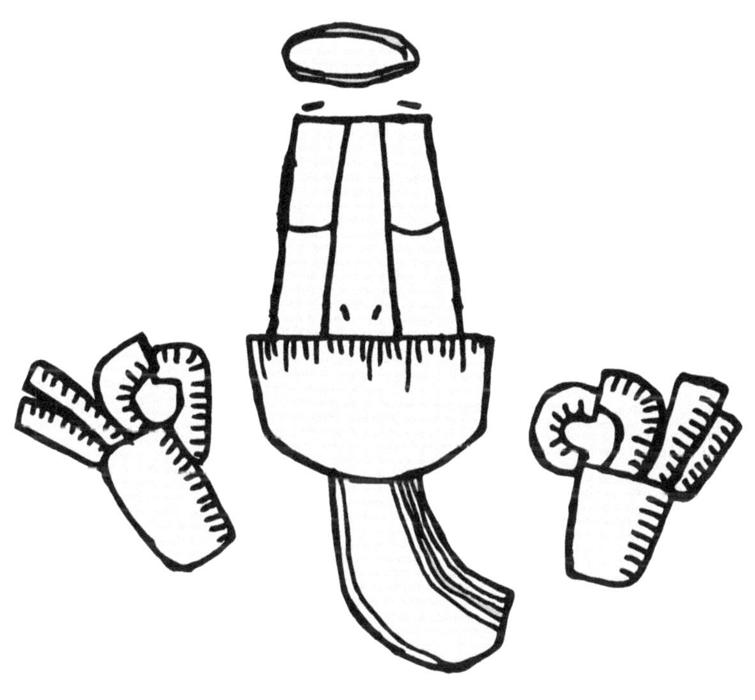

I WAS BORN ARISTORTOISE. I CHANGED MY NAME TO ARISTURTLE. I FEEL QUITE THE ROCK STAR NOW.

IF I KEEP GOING I WILL GET THERE.

WHERE DOES WISDOM COME FROM I ASKED ?
LOOK WITHIN CAME THE ANSWER. SO THIS IS WHY I GO
INSIDE MY SHELL EVER SO OFTEN

THERE IS A BIRD THAT SITS ON MY SHELL FROM TIME TO TIME. I THINK IT FEELS COMFORTABLE WITH ME TRAVELLING SO SLOWLY.

MY COUSINS ARE FABULOUS SWIMMERS. I WOULD SINK LIKE A STONE IF I WENT INTO THE WATER. STRANGE WE ARE EVEN RELATED.

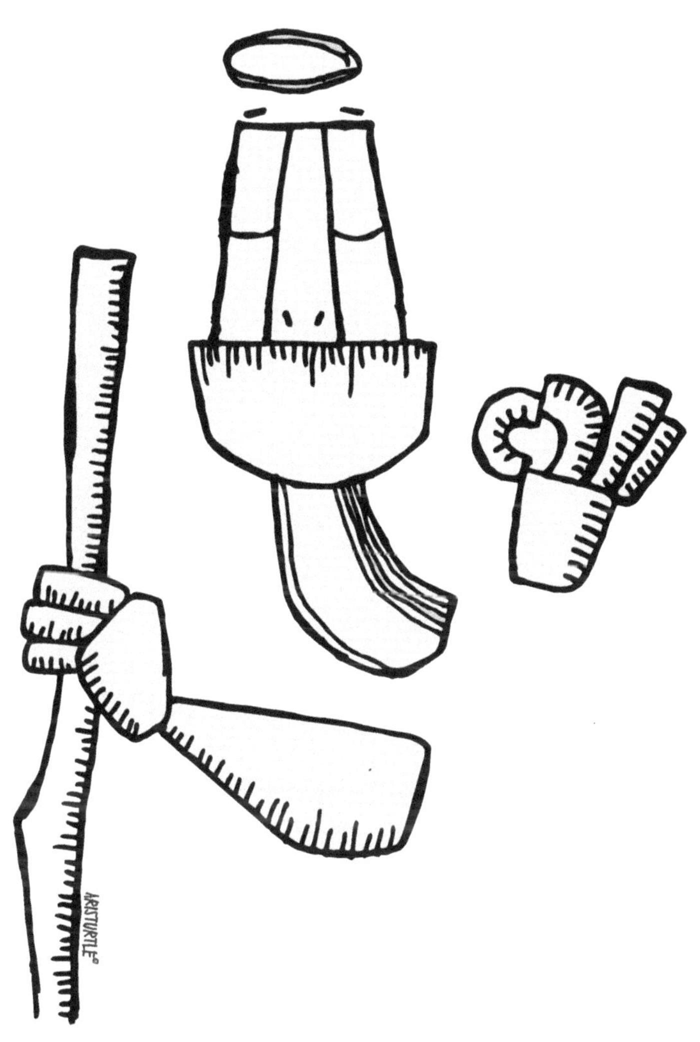

WHAT IS PATIENCE I WAS ASKED.
I HAD TO THINK ABOUT THAT FOR AWHILE.

LATER THAT YEAR I ANSWERED. PATIENCE IS NOTHING
MORE THAN WAITING FOR TIME TO CATCH UP WITH YOU.

I WAS TAUGHT BY A PLATYPUS.
EVERYONE CALLED HIM PLATO FOR SHORT.

PLATO LIKED CAVES FOR SOME REASON.
HE WROTE ABOUT ONE TOO.

WHO'S TO SAY THAT SMARTER PEOPLE ARE FASTER?
THEY DON'T HANG AROUND LONG ENOUGH TO FIND OUT.

I WOULDN'T HAVE LASTED AS LONG AS I HAVE
IF I HADN'T STOPPED NOW AND THEN TO CHEW
SOME OF THE FLOWERS.

LIFE IS TOO SHORT TO HOLD ANY GRUDGES. ASK ME.
I HAVE BEEN AROUND FOR A 100 YEARS OR SO.

I WAS IN LOVE ONCE. I THINK SHE LIKED ME TOO.
SHE WAS A TURTLE. AND I WAS A TORTOISE. CHANGING
MY NAME DIDN'T HELP.

www.ingramcontent.com/pod-product-compliance
Lightning Source LLC
Chambersburg PA
CBHW041214140726
48010CB00030B/177